The Buildings Of the University

© Philip Opher
Based on material originally Compiled by
Keith Denham and Alberto Yarza

With thanks to Marny Leech, David Eynon, Valerie Opher and Aya Matsumoto

First published 2007

THE ROUTE

This guide is one of a series on various aspects of Oxford. The route goes round the small area in the centre of the city, in which the University started, and which still contains its principal buildings. Many aspects of the history and design of the buildings, in this world-famous environment, are explained using photographs, plans and old prints. The guide has been prepared for visitors to the city and for interested citizens. The recommended route starts and finishes at the High Street entrance to St Mary's Church. Directions are given in the margin. We hope that this guide will add to the interest and pleasure of your walk and provide a valuable record of your visit.

Faden's map of 1789

Sheldonian Theatre

The Clarendon Building

Former Indian Institute

Schools Quadrangle

Schools Quadrangle

Hertford College

Exeter College

Radcliffe Camera

All Souls College Library

Brasenose College

Saint Mary's Church

All Souls College Chapel

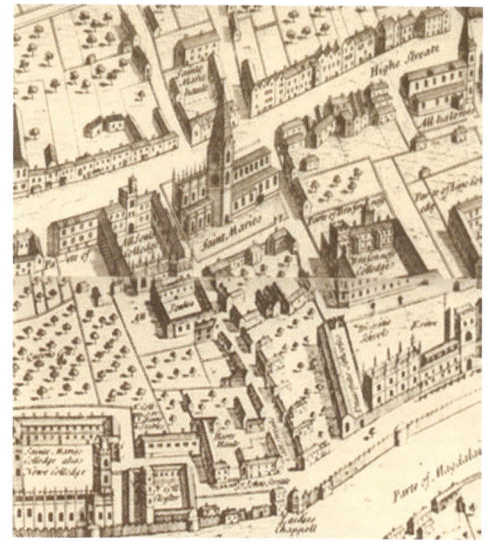

Agas's map of 1578 (re drawn by Whittlesey 1728) South at top
Note: city wall

Hollars map of 1643
South at top
Note: Schools Quadrangle and buildings on line of city wall before Sheldonian

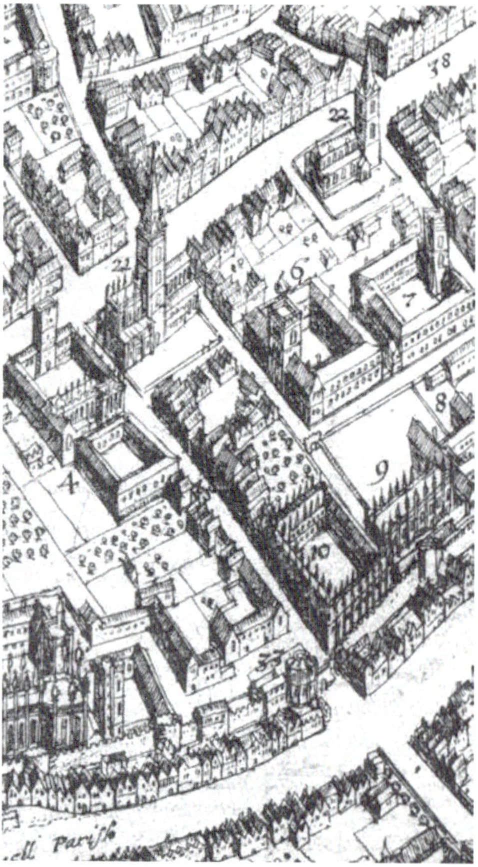

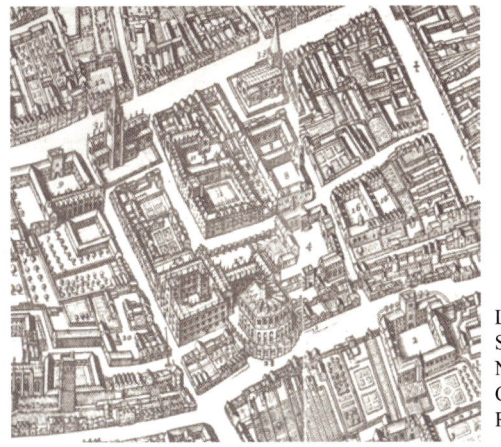

Loggan's map of 1675
South at top
Note: Sheldonian before Clarendon building and Radcliffe Camera

INTRODUCTION

OXFORD University does not have a self-contained campus. Most of the colleges and the University facilities are spread around the City, integrated with commercial and domestic developments. However in one area, just off the High Street, a magnificent group of buildings forms the *Heart of the University*. This guide examines that area, describing the history and architecture of the buildings and the urban spaces they create.

From its early beginnings, sometime in the 12th century, all the activities of the University took place in St Mary's Church. The University's governing body, the Congregation, met there. The University Administration and Library were contained there and, until the middle of the 17th century, University degrees were awarded inside the Church.

All Souls College and, later, Brasenose College, were founded close to the Church, linking it to the first of the University's own buildings; the Divinity School and the Schools Quadrangle. At the same time, towards the end of the 15th century, the University Library outgrew the room in St Mary's and was moved to space above the Divinity School.

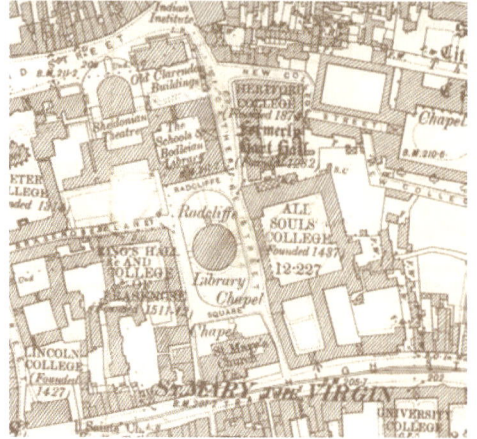

Ordnance Survey map 1898 North at top showing area much as it is today

Later, the Library took over all the teaching-room there, as it gradually grew into the world-famous Bodleian Library. The University Administration ultimately moved into the Convocation House. When degree ceremonies grew too large and too rowdy for St. Mary's, the Sheldonian Theatre was built, in 1669, for these ceremonies. In 1715 the Clarendon Building was built for the University Press, on a site facing Broad Street. All that remained to complete this remarkable area was the construction of the magnificent Radcliffe Camera in 1745 and, in the 19th century, buildings for Hertford College.

Thus one of the world's great urban settings was not a piece of formal urban planning, but rather the result of six hundred years of academic and architectural evolution. Nevertheless, the area is remarkable for its overall unity, while embracing a series of complex and varied urban spaces and a variety of building uses and architectural styles. It provides an excellent example of a typically English approach to urban design: formal without being strictly geometric; dignified without being ponderous, and made up of buildings whose architects treated the strict rules of style in a delightfully free and relaxed way.

Photograph opposite:
Tenor Placido Domingo on the way to the Sheldonian to receive an honarary degree in 2005

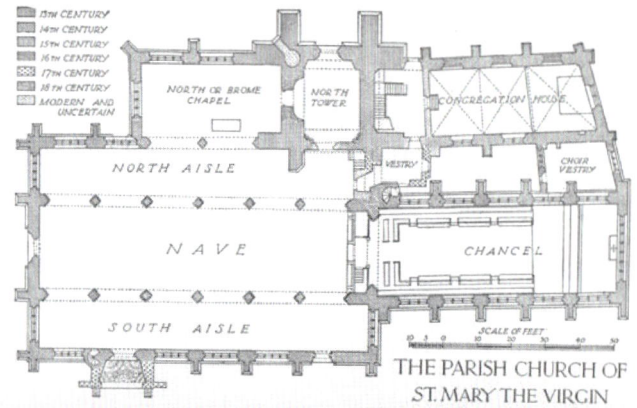

THE PARISH CHURCH OF
ST. MARY THE VIRGIN

Saint Mary's Church

The walk starts in the High Street about 100 meters east of Carfax, the centre of the city.

The University Church of St Mary the Virgin, which is also Oxford's Parish Church, is easily identified in the High Street by its soaring spire, dominating the scene. This spire is one of the highest of any parish church in the country and is certainly one of the most spectacular.

Like most other English churches, St Mary's has been altered and enlarged many times. The plan shows that that only the tower and spire date from the 13th.century. In the northeast corner a small addition, built in the 14th century and now a delightful café, was the first home of the University's governing body, the Congregation, and of the University Chest, its administration. Above the present-day café the University's first Library, the beginnings of the Bodleian, was founded. (Also here, the world-wide charity Oxfam was started in the 1940s). Most of the rest of the church, the nave, its aisles and the chancel (or choir), is 15th century.

Nineteenth-century architectural historians divided English Gothic into three periods: Early English (1180-1300), Decorated (1300-1370), and Perpendicular (1370-1550). St Mary's is a fine example of this latter style - tall, slender columns widely spaced, large windows, and an overall impression of lightness and delicacy.

Saint Mary's Church Porch

The delightful exterior facing the High has large windows, carved corbels and numerous decorative pinnacles, all late Gothic in detail. The elaborate entrance porch is therefore a great surprise. This porch, built in 1637, is in the Baroque (meaning, literally, overwrought, florid, or extravagantly ornamented) style which was all the rage in Italy at this time when, after two hundred years, architects and their clients had become bored with the strictly 'Classical' rules of the early Renaissance. In England this kind of design was strikingly, and scandalously, new. The sensuously twisted Corinthian columns, the volutes, the broken pediment ending in scrolls, and the shell-topped niche above the statue of the Virgin with angels perched on either side must have shocked local people, only recently acquainted with the Renaissance from the few elements that were half-heartedly introduced into the Schools Quadrangle (Page 19).

Some people would have known that this porch was directly inspired by the canopy

Saint Mary's Church Porch
continued

which Bernini had just had built over the high altar in the Pope's Church of St Peter in Rome. King Charles I had recently bought a painting of St Peter's by Raphael (the Raphael cartoons are now in the Victoria and Albert Museum, London). The Virgin's statue would have confirmed popular suspicion that this was a piece of Roman Catholic propaganda. The design of the porch was later used as evidence against Charles' Archbishop, William Laud, after the king's execution, at a time, during the Commonwealth, when Roman sympathies led to the execution of many Catholics, including Laud.

The ceiling of the porch is a Gothic fan vault, illustrating how uncertain local architect Nicholas Stone was about this new style of architecture., Oxford had to wait another thirty years for its first fully-fledged Renaissance building, Wren's Sheldonian theatre(page 24).

One of the most remarkable things about the porch is the way that it harmonises with the rest of the church. Perhaps this was because the porch was built of similar stone, which, mellowing over the years, has become the same colour and texture as the rest of the building. Such a striking contrast between new and old would nowadays provoke furious objections.

Saint Mary's Church
Interior

The first impression on entering the church is of a gloriously-tall interior, flooded with light. The characteristically graceful perpendicular columns of the nave support a row of clerestory windows below a timber roof resting on projecting corbels. The recesses between the windows, intended for statues, were never filled. Beyond the spectacular free-standing modern organ, the chancel, lined with beautiful old pews, is lit by the huge south windows noted outside. Generally the interior is plain and simple. Apart from some memorials there is little decoration. Much of the window glass is clear and if there had been any Medieval stained glass it has all gone, replaced by Victorian windows. From the back of the early-19th century gallery at the west end of the nave it is possible to get an unusually close look at the stained glass in the largest of the windows and to see how it is put together.

Apart from its architecture, St Mary's, like many old buildings, is linked with people and events from the past. Bishops Cranmer, Latimer and Ridley were tried here. Later, at the foot of the last column in the nave, a platform was built (the damage done to the column is still visible). Archbishop Cranmer, author of the prayer book, standing on this platform, was expected to

Saint Mary's Church Interior. Continued

recant his belief in the Reformation and to rejoin the Church of Rome. To the fury of his prosecutors Cranmer changed his mind at the last moment and was taken straight from the church to be burnt at the stake in Broad Street. Not long after when the Protestants were again in power, the Catholic Edmund Champion's preaching here lead to his Catholic martyrdom. Many years later Charles Wesley the founder of theMethodist Church, also preached in St Mary's. In the 19th-century William Keble expounded doctrines here which inspired the Oxford Movement and Henry Newman (one time Vicar and later Cardinal) preached here, before joining the Church of Rome, and provoked still-unresolved divisions among Anglicans.

Saint Mary's Church tower

Tickets to climb the tower (fee £2.50 with concessions) are obtained from the friendly staff in the gift shop. The climb is quite strenuous towards the top.

The tower and spire of St Mary's, 46m (150ft) high, is best seen from the garden (and summer cafe) on the north side of the church. From here the beautiful, elaborate stone carvings, especially at the corners at the junction of the tower and the spire, can be appreciated. The masonry was twice restored in the 19th century (some of the original Medieval figures are now in New College Cloister). The climb to the outside gallery below the spire is very rewarding. On the way up there is a close view of the

gargoyles and pinnacles of the nave roof. From the gallery there are some spectacular views over the city.

Looking down to the north, the view is dominated by the magnificent Radcliffe Camera. This is also a good place to appreciate the layout of some of the colleges, and to note the overall unity of the city, slightly shattered by the intrusion of some 20th-century buildings. The longer views of the green landscape, some of which comes very close to the city centre, give an idea of the size and character of Oxford.

Descend the stairs and leave the church through the lobby of the north porch at the base of the tower and enter Radcliffe Square.

Radcliffe Square

The buildings of Radcliffe Square create one of the finest architectural groups in England. On the west side of the square is Brasenose College, its Chapel with a magnificent east window, a mixture of Gothic and Classical detail and some elaborate carving. The long façade of the College Library has an unusual Venetian Oriel window. Beyond Brasenose entrance gatehouse the high, rustic stone wall enclosing Exeter College garden completes the enclosure.

The north side is dominated by the Schools Quadrangle, a beautifully simple repetitive design with big square windows and plain panels of stone. All Souls College, a mixture

of Gothic and *Gothick*-revival architecture, fills the east side of the Square. This varied collection of buildings is a worthy setting for the strictly classical Radcliffe Camera which dominates the whole space. The square has recently been re-cobbled. The railings round the Camera, removed as part of the war effort in 1940, have been replaced and the immaculate lawn reseeded. Now, usually free of parked vehicles, the square is a worthy setting for fine architecture.

Radcliffe Camera

The Camera (from the Latin *Camera* - room), was built with money bequeathed by Dr Radcliffe, a famous physician, on his death in 1714. At the time the centre of the Square was a jumble of Medieval houses. Nicholas Hawksmoor, the joint architect of Blenheim Palace and many Oxford buildings (including the Clarendon building and part of All Souls in this area), made radical proposals to turn this part of the city into a grand, classically-inspired, University Forum. Like most English grand plans, Hawksmoor's proposals were never carried out, although they did included a design for a circular library, suggesting several places for it within the Forum. However, seven years later, the trustees decided to hold an architectural competition, inviting Christopher Wren, John Vanbrugh (of Blenheim), James Gibbs, and Hawksmoor himself to submit plans. Only Hawksmoor and Gibbs did so, and fourteen years after that Gibbs' design was selected in preference to Hawksmoor's. The Camera's foundation stone was laid in 1737. The building was finished in 1749, thirty-five years after Dr Radcliffe's death. The Interior, a single space with galleries on a first floor below the dome, was originally an independent library (and the place for parties and banquets) but is now part of the Bodleian.

Radcliffe Camera continued

Gibbs' design achieved one of a Renaissance architect's ambitions - a free-standing circular building surmounted by a dome. His ground floor, built of wide-jointed stones, known as *rustication*, was originally an open, vaulted space, like a Medieval market hall, used for informal meetings and discussions (and lovers' trysts). It was not enclosed until the end of the 19th century. The main two-storey rotunda, 31 meters in diameter, is ringed with pairs of massive Corinthian columns just attached to the walls and topped by a deep cornice and balustrade, decorated with stone balls where the *Goths* would have put pinnacles. The dome is the building's crowning glory. The building is entirely Classical and therefore unique in the square, yet in harmony with the buildings that surround it. As with the Baroque porch of St Mary's, the use of the same type of stone provides a unifying element.

Classical design strives after an order based on symmetry about a common axis, which the surrounding buildings do not have. The circular form with no single axis or principal facade solves a difficult urban design problem. The Camera relates equally to the varied informal elevations of the pre-existing buildings. Its position in the centre, preventing views across the square, helps unify this wonderful urban ensemble.

Brasenose College

Proceed to the west side of the square and enter the gateway of Brasenose College.

The name of this College is a bit of a mystery. It is derived from the bronze mask or 'brazen nose' at the head of the great oak entrance doors. The nose was first mentioned in 1534, thirty three years after the first quadrangle was built. A hundred years later this quad was altered by the addition on the roof of the rooms with dormer windows, a typical way by which many of the Oxford colleges expanded their accommodations. Another typical feature of Oxford is the embattled or *crenellated* parapets seen on the entrance tower. This is an architectural detail of the Tudor period, arising from the need in earlier times to defend buildings. The feature lingered on as a status symbol and decorative motif and was revived again by nineteenth-century architects.

The brazen nose

Seen from the back of the Quad, the huge dome of the Radcliffe Camera looms over the entrance tower, with the spire of St Mary's to the right. This view emphasises the domestic scale of the typical college quadrangle. The most spectacular building at Brasenose is the College Chapel, built in 1656, a Gothick/Classical mélange with a magnificent fan-vault, cheaply achieved with plaster imitating stone.

Schools Quadrangle and the Divinity School

This whole group of buildings on the north side of Radcliffe Square is now part of the Bodleian Library, arguably Oxford's single greatest treasure. The Schools Quadrangle, originally housed all the subjects taught at the University at the time it was built in 1613. The external facades, including the gateway in Catte Street, are remarkably plain; a fortress-like block of Gothic masonry, topped with decorative pinnacles and crenellations. This was one of the first - and remains one of the largest - of the buildings of the University. Although neither grand nor ponderous, it is suitably sober and dignified.

From Brasenose College, cross the north-west corner of the Square and proceed towards the Schools Quadrangle of the Bodleian Library.

The inside of the Quad is a delight. Taller and narrower than the usual residential quad, it is still light and open. The names of the various schools are still indicated on the doors on the ground floor; Logic; Music; Astronomy and Rhetoric; Natural Philosophy; Medicine; Moral Philosophy and Grammar and History. At first only the top floor was part of the Bodleian, but it now occupies the whole building.

The official entrance to the quadrangle is via the gateway on the east elevation. It is also possible to enter through the tunnel under the building on the south elevation

The facades within the Quad are more decorative than those outside. The west wall is delicately panelled and, dominating the whole space is the remarkable entrance

tower, opposite. This is one of Oxford's most spectacular architectural compositions, in a style which is both Classical and Gothic, a mixture known as 'Jacobean', after King James I, who made frequent visits to Oxford. His statue sits in a circular niche in the fourth storey, below his family coat of arms. Apparently James was not keen on the bright colours in which the statue was originally painted.

This tower introduced Oxford to the five Orders of Classical, Renaissance architecture, already fully mature in Italy and France but new in early 17th-century England. From bottom to top, there is Tuscan, Roman Doric, Ionic, Corinthian, and finally a composite of Corinthian and Ionic Orders. These Orders are all surrounded by Gothic carving. Above them are Gothic towers and pinnacles.

The Schools Quadrangle was built as an addition to the most important school of the University- the Divinity School, which is the oldest lecture room in Oxford. It was built between 1420 and 1483, and designed as a single story. During construction, in 1444, Duke Humfrey, the brother of King Henry V, gave money for a library, which now bears his name, to be built above the

The Divinity School

The Divinity School, entered through the Bodleian Shop, is included on the Bodleian tour, for which a fee is charged. Details of times and prices: E mail tours@bodley.ox.ac.uk

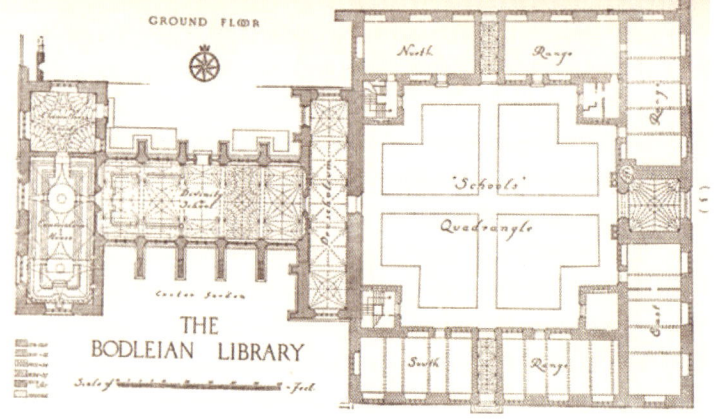

The Divinity School Continued

Divinity School. The original outside wall of the building is opposite the shop entrance, which is itself behind the fine bronze statue of the Earl of Pembroke in the Quad.

The interior of the Divinity School is one of the most remarkable rooms in England. The ceiling is a spectacular example of late Gothic *lierne vaulting* with pendants. This vault, which represents the ultimate in the constructional skill of its Gothic builders, had to be strengthened to carry the enormously heavy load of books, once the Library was added above. The vault, together with the room's large window, is typical of the late Perpendicular period and is contemporary with the nave and chancel of St Mary's church.

The complexity and beauty of the countless bosses (which originated as the *keystone* of the vault) is amazing. These bosses, at all the junctions of the web of ribs, are elaborately decorated with figures, inscriptions, coats of arms or monograms. Many celebrate Thomas and John Kemp - Bishop of London and Archbishop of Canterbury, and William Waynflete, who founded Magdalen College. One boss has the letters "W.O.", possibly the initials of William Orchard, one of the architects of the building.

Most of the books in Duke Humfrey's library were on Roman Catholic theology and were removed during Henry VIII's Reformation. Thomas Bodley not only restocked this library, but also added the Arts End, above the present shop, in 1610 and the Selden End, above the Convocation House (for University meetings), in 1632. More details of the whole of the Bodleian Library are in a companion volume in this series: *Oxford Libraries*.

The Bodleian Library

The Bodleian Library is open only to scholars who have registered as Readers. However parts of the library are included on guided tours

Take the passage under north side of the Schools Quadrangle leads into a paved area outside the Sheldonian Theatre and the Clarendon building.

The position of the city wall is indicated on the paving of this urban space. The building on the left is the Sheldonian Theatre, built for the *Encaenia,* the ceremony confirring of University degrees, previously held in Saint Mary's Church. The massive Clarendon Building encloses the north side. These buildings both use the Classical architectural language derived from ancient Greece and Rome. The Sheldonian was built in 1669, and the Clarendon Building in 1713, by which time the Classical Renaissance had become firmly established in England.

The Sheldonian Theatre

Tours of the Sheldonian during the day are only possible when there are no ceremonies or rehearsals. A fee is charged

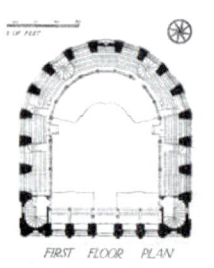

The Sheldonian is one of Sir Christopher Wren's first designs. He was at the time Professor of Astronomy and had no training as an architect. Like many amateurs at the time, he copied his design from a book by an Italian, Sebastiano Serlio, which included drawings of the Roman Theatre of Marcellus. The main façade of Wren's building is opposite an entrance door to the Divinity School (which he also designed, but in *Gothick,* to match the rest of that building). This is very clearly the building's front: its less formal arcaded back sticks out like the stern of a ship into Broad Street. During University ceremonies the principal participants walk in procession from the

Convocation House at the end of the Divinity School to the Sheldonian (named after Bishop Sheldon, who paid for the building), hence the reason why Wren's main façade is almost hidden away. This is not regretted by some critics, who find the details of the design - for instance the relationship of the giant pilasters to the pediment - awkward and amateurish.

Unlike the Roman model, which needed only a temporary roof awning using ropes and canvas (represented on Robert Streeter's ceiling painting), Wren's building had to have a permanent roof. To avoid internal columns, which would restrict the view, he developed an idea of a Professor of Geometry (Wallis) for a lattice structure for the clear span of 70 feet. Wren was rightly very proud of this and gave a lecture about it as a founder member of the Royal Society. The interior is best experienced at one of the many concerts which now take place in the Sheldonian. Although seats are uncomfortable, there is plenty of time to

enjoy the wonderful interior and some interesting 'furniture'. At other times, it is possible to climb up to the *lantern* for *views* over the city. The route up to the *lantern* passes through a roof space above the ceiling, where the huge timber trusses, necessary to span the space beneath, can be seen.

Museum of Science

The Museum of Science to the west of the Sheldonian was started a few years after the Theatre. Not only was this the first home of the Ashmoleian Museum but it was also first purpose-built Museum in England. It is now houses a fascinating collection of scientific instruments. The main façade, facing Broad Street, is like a typical grand town house of the period. On the side facing the Theatre there is a richly-carved ceremonial doorway to the Museum (never used). This doorway has a semi-circular pediment which makes an interesting comparison to St Mary's entrance porch (page 9), illustrating the variety of Renaissance design.

Wren's witty and probably unique idea for the screen to Broad Street, the giant heads, are sometimes called 'the Emperors'. The heads have been replaced several times, most recently in 1972. They are one of Oxfords most famous and most photographed oddities.

The Clarendon Building

The most northerly building in the University complex is the Clarendon Building, erected in 1715 for the Oxford University Press as their printing works, which had outgrown its first home in the basement and roof space of the Sheldonian.

Lord Clarendon wrote the *History of the Great Rebellion,* an 18th-century bestseller, which made enough profit to pay for the building. The Press remained here until the end of the 19th-century, when it moved to its present home in Jericho. The building is now the Bodleian registry but some OUP books are still published under the Clarendon imprint.

Nicholas Hawksmoor designed the building while working at Blenheim Palace under his teacher (and later partner) Sir John Vanbrugh. Vanbrugh's epitaph was *'Lie heavy on him earth for he hath laid many a heavy load on thee'.* Looking at the Clarendon Building, it is obvious that Hawksmoor was a good pupil.

The two main elevations of the building have huge Tuscan columns, rising through two storeys to support a pediment. On the Broad Street side these columns stand free of the building, at the top of a flight of steps,

creating a massive entrance portico to the group to the south. On the south elevation similar columns are attached to the building. All the details, particularly the deeply-recessed windows, are heavy and largely undecorated, in sombre contrast to Wren's building. Although it has none of the frivolity of the Italian Baroque, (viz. the porch of St Mary's Page 9) Vanbrugh's and Hawksmoor's buildings are regarded as English versions of the Baroque style. The delicate wrought-iron gates, which close off the passage passing through the building, presents a contrast to the architecture

Catte Street (Townscape)

Buildings in cities are rarely seen individually. Usually they form continuous sequences. This arrangement of buildings in towns is sometimes called *townscape,* the art of ensemble, experienced with *serial vision.* The idea was first explored by the planner Thomas Sharp, in *Oxford Replanned,* published in 1948, illustrating his words with drawings along the route from Broad Street to St Mary's, Sharp wrote:

"As we approach the Bodleian from Catte Street there is nothing to be seen but its noble cube. Advancing we see first the Rotunda, then the spire of St Mary's, then the dome of the Radcliffe coming into view. As this vast circular bulk separates

from the Bodleian, the tower of St Mary's also emerges. Despite the fact that each of these three buildings is in its own way as sophisticated a piece of architecture as there is, the experience is elemental beyond the power of words or photographs to describe. Cube, cylinder and cone are suddenly juxtaposed, or rather suddenly deploy, the one from the other with a result that is architecturally speaking sensational."

Sharp's sequence remains the same today. It starts at the former Indian Institute building, which closes the vista along Broad Street at the corner of Catte Street. The building, now a library, is a pleasing mixture of Oriental Baroque on the rounded corner and Jacobean on the rest. Carved elephants and an Indian cupola add a touch of humour to the design. Before the city wall was removed, Smith Gate stood here and, as usual at a city gate, a small chapel stood just inside it. The present octagonal building is Victorian, but a small Medieval sculpture of the Annunciation remains above the door; a precious and delightful survivor.

Hertford College

Hertford College, which was re-founded here in the late 19th-century, now fills most of the east side of the street up to All Souls. The buildings are all by Sir Thomas Jackson, who had the brilliant idea of connecting the college with a bridge across New College Lane, an Anglicised version of the famous "Bridge of Sighs" in Venice. This bridge is now another of the most frequently-photographed features of all Oxford buildings. Jackson's buildings for Hertford are in various architectural styles – Gothick, Palladian Jacobean. He designed many other Oxford buildings at the turn of the 19th century, firing shots in several directions in that battle of styles which was then at its height (and which so disgusted the puritanical 20th century architects of the Modern Movement).

Walk further along Catte Street to look at the buildings on the east side of Radcliffe Square.

The 'Bridge of Sighs' on May morning

All Souls College

All Souls College fills the whole east side of Radcliffe Square. The college, founded in 1438, is different from other ancient colleges. It does not take undergraduates, but is made up of visiting fellows from Britain and overseas who spend a short time here and supervise graduate students. It has a long list of distinguished members. The original building, South Quadrangle, is entered from the High Street. The west façade of the Chapel faces the Square. North Quadrangle, opposite the Radcliffe Camera, was designed by Nicholas Hawksmoor at the beginning of the 18th century. Hawksmoor, like Wren before him, turned his hand from Baroque *Gothick* when he thought it appropriate. Hawksmoor considered his design in the context of his

abortive plans for the University Forum, but also had to take into account the existing All Souls Chapel. The result is an extremely original design which combines Classical symmetry with *Gothick* detail. The west side of the quadrangle facing Radcliffe Square is a covered colonnade with a domed entrance-pavilion, creating an interesting screen between the two spaces.

Through the wonderful (but rarely used) entrance gates there is a glimpse of Hawksmoor's twin towers and of a large sundial, designed by Wren, high up on the library wall.

The Codrington Library fills the north side of North Quadrangle, with a façade facing on the Square. Built in 1716, it echoes the facade of the Chapel at the other end of the colonnade and is thus a revival of Perpendicular Gothic, complete with crenellations and pinnacles. However, behind the tracery of the library's big window, it is possible to see a silhouette of a Venetian window, a favourite Renaissance motif, on the inside. Thus Hawksmoor literally had it both ways - Gothic outside, Classical in - a case of hedging the architectural bets.

The walk ends back at the High Street at the eastern end of Saint Mary's church.